Steel Rigg © Northern Horizons   Willowford Bridge A   orizons

This set of walks and itineraries presents some of the best walking in Hadrian's Wall Country from South Shields to Ravenglass. You can concentrate on the Wall itself or sample some of the hidden gems just waiting to be discovered – the choice is yours. Make a day of it by visiting some of the many historic sites and attractions along the walks and dwell awhile for refreshment at the cafés, pubs and restaurants that you will come across. Just pick the walks that suit you and enjoy yourself!

Key to map

Approximate line of Hadrian's Wall World Heritage Site	▬
Wall Remains	🏰
Major Roman Site	●
Tourist Information Centre (year-round)	🇮
Tourist Information Centre (seasonal)	Ⓘ
Hadrian's Wall Path National Trail	▬
Hadrian's Cycleway	▬
Motorway	▬
A Roads (Major)	▬
A Roads (Minor)	▬
B Roads	▬
Minor Road	▬
Parking	🅿
Rail station*	●
Tyne & Wear Metro station	Ⓜ
Airport	✈
Ferry port	⛴

* Only rail stations relevant to the line of the World Heritage Site are shown. Major conurbations (eg Newcastle upon Tyne, Carlisle) have rail stations but these are not indicated for the sake of clarity.

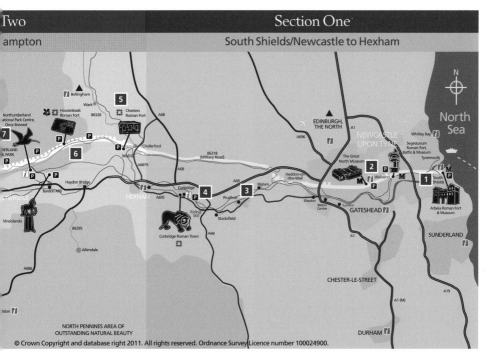

Two   **Section One**

ampton   **South Shields/Newcastle to Hexham**

© Crown Copyright and database right 2011. All rights reserved. Ordnance Survey Licence number 100024900.

"The most complex and best preserved of the frontiers of the Roman Empire"

Hadrian's Wall was originally inscribed as a World Heritage Site (WHS) in 1987 as the most complex and best preserved of the frontiers of the Roman Empire. Today, Hadrian's Wall is part of the transnational Frontiers of the Roman Empire WHS, inscribed in 2005 and currently comprising Hadrian's Wall, the German Limes and the Antonine Wall in Scotland.

Hadrian's Wall is a very sensitive place, a fragile piece of our heritage. Almost everywhere that you walk is archaeologically important, so we all have a responsibility to make sure that the surviving remains are preserved for future generations.

As well as the visible archaeology (both masonry and earthworks) that you can see there is much more buried beneath the very paths that run alongside the Wall. We want to avoid damage and erosion to the ancient monument and the best way of doing this is by maintaining the path beside the Wall as a healthy grass surface.

West of Aesica Fort (Great Chesters)
© Natural England / Graeme Peacock

Approach to Birdoswald © Natural England / Graeme Peacock

CONSERVATION TIPS:

- **PLEASE DO NOT** stand or climb on Hadrian's Wall.
- Ditches, mounds and other earthwork features are archaeologically sensitive and protected by a grass surface. To help reduce the wear and tear on the ground, please walk side by side instead of single file and try to avoid walking in worn lines. This really does help.
- The ground surface that protects the archaeology is most vulnerable in wet winter conditions (November to April). Circular walks have been designed so that walkers can experience the World Heritage Site, whilst limiting their impact on archaeological remains.
- Take special care not to damage, destroy or remove natural or historical features.
- In order to protect the archaeology, organisers of large groups should contact us for advice on special arrangements.
- Running races are **NOT** encouraged along the National Trail. Contact us for advice on alternative routes, tel 01434 609700

Banks © Heptinstall   *Cawfield Crags* © Northern Horizons   *Birdoswald* © Heptinstall

The Wall's own country code, Every Footstep Counts

This code was devised by the National Trail in partnership with all of the projects and organisations associated with the World Heritage Site. It suggests tips on how visitors can help us to look after the Wall for them and future generations.

 1. Never climb up or walk on top of Hadrian's Wall.

2. During the wet winter months the ground is waterlogged and this is when the risk of damage to the monument is greatest. Instead you could walk one of the alternative circular walks close by. The Trail's Passport season is between May and October only.

 3. Use public transport, including the Hadrian's Wall Country Bus, wherever you can.

4. You can support the people living and working in the World Heritage Site by staying nearby whenever you can and using shops, restaurants and pubs in the area.

 5. Take any litter away with you and never light fires.

6. Close all gates behind you unless it is clear that the farmer needs the gate to be left open.

7. Follow the path, signed with the National Trail Acorns and coloured arrows.

8. Help to take pressure off the Wall itself by visiting a Roman fort as part of the journey.

Cawfields © Northern Horizons

Walkers, Dogs and Farm Animals

Cattle are naturally protective towards their young and can attack both people and dogs.

Keep to the path where possible, however, do your best to avoid walking through herds of cattle and livestock. Farm animals can behave unpredictably if you get too close, especially if they're with their young – so give them plenty of space.

Always keep your dog under close control. Your dog can scare or harm farm animals. Keep it on a lead around livestock, but let go if chased by cattle.

Hadrian's Wall Path National Trail

Solway Coast © Heptinstall

Hadrian's Wall Path National Trail is an unbroken 84-mile signposted footpath stretching coast-to-coast and crossing England from Wallsend in the east to Bowness-on-Solway in the west.

It passes through some of England's most beautiful and dynamic landscapes – the forces that shaped our island's geography have left behind a kaleidoscope of scenery – from rolling fields and rugged moorland to the vibrant cities of Newcastle upon Tyne and Carlisle.

You do not have to walk all of the Trail in one go, although many people do; it is just as popular as a short-stay destination, perhaps walking a section over a long weekend, or for a day walk.

If you do decide to walk the Trail please note that its popular passport scheme operates from 1st May to 31st October only. Collecting all seven stamps in the passport from the stamping stations enables you to buy the exclusive Hadrian's Wall Path completion badge and certificate.

The Summer Passport was introduced in 2003, the year the Trail was officially opened. One of the most important reasons why it came into being was the need to promote the conservation of the World Heritage Site. Walking the Trail during the

Gradient Profile

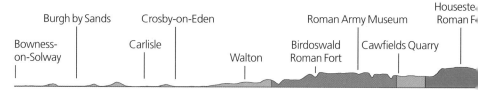

Bowness-on-Solway • Burgh by Sands • Carlisle • Crosby-on-Eden • Walton • Birdoswald Roman Fort • Roman Army Museum • Cawfields Quarry • Houseste Roman F

National Trail Map

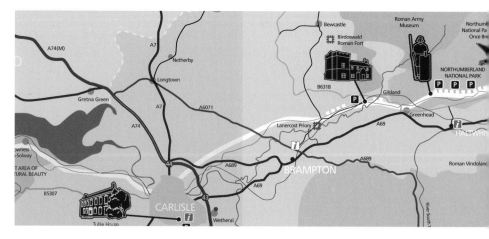

Whinshields Crags © Northern Horizons   *Castle Nick* © Roger Clegg   *Housesteads Fort* © Roger Clegg

normally drier months helps to conserve the underlying archaeology when the soils tend to withstand more wear-and-tear. We also know that many people love to collect the stamps and to keep their fully stamped Passport as a great souvenir of their achievement!

During the winter months we recommend you walk instead some of the many footpaths in Hadrian's Wall Country – some of which are featured in this book.

National Trail Maps, Guides and Passports are available to purchase from the Hadrian's Wall Country Online Shop at hadrians-wall.org

Key to Gradient Profile

- Easy walk suitable for wheelchair users
- Easy walk unsuitable for wheelchair users
- More difficult walk – wear boots
- Very strenuous walk

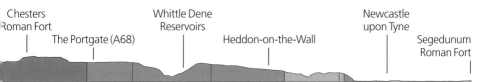

Chesters Roman Fort | The Portgate (A68) | Whittle Dene Reservoirs | Heddon-on-the-Wall | Newcastle upon Tyne | Segedunum Roman Fort

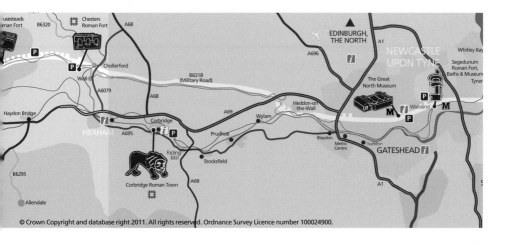

© Crown Copyright and database right 2011. All rights reserved. Ordnance Survey Licence number 100024900.

Three walking itineraries incorporating the National Trail

Carlisle Castle © English Heritage/D&H Photographers

We have put together some suggestions for walking sections of the National Trail, using Newcastle or Carlisle as your base. The following itineraries have been designed for the summer months, taking advantage of the seasonal AD122 Hadrian's Wall Bus, and allow time to take in the landscapes and visit some of the Roman sites and attractions.

A 5-day itinerary starting in Carlisle
(3 walking days)

Walk the Cumbrian section of the Trail in 3 days. Use Carlisle as your initial base for 2 nights before you walk further east.

Day 1: Arrive in Carlisle and leave your bags in your accommodation. Explore the city's parks, cultural quarter and museums.

Day 2: Take the No 93 service bus to either Bowness (15 miles) or, if you prefer a shorter walk, to Burgh-by-Sands (7 miles) and walk back to Carlisle.

Day 3: Walk from Carlisle to Walton (11 miles) and stay in Walton.

Day 4: Walk from Walton to Gilsland (8 miles). Stay in Gilsland or take the AD122 Hadrian's Wall Bus back into Carlisle for a final evening there.

Day 5: Last-minute sight-seeing and souvenir shopping in Carlisle before returning home.

Bowness-on-Solway © Natural England / Graeme Peacock

TRIP HIGHLIGHTS:
- Views across the Solway marshes into Scotland
- Port Carlisle's historic canal basin
- Drumburgh Moss National Nature Reserve
- Carlisle Castle (English Heritage)
- Carlisle Cathedral
- Tullie House Museum
- Lanercost Priory (English Heritage) – 1/2 mile south of the Trail
- 360° panoramas
- Hadrian's Wall, Milecastles, Turrets, Vallum and Wall ditch
- Birdoswald Roman Fort and Museum (English Heritage)
- Award-winning footbridge across River Irthing gorge

SOLWAY TIDE TIMES:
Check Tide Boards or visit www.tidetimes.org.uk/silloth (flooding may occur at heights of 9 metres and above). GMT add 1 hour, BST add 2 hours

Birdoswald © Heptinstall   Tyne bridges © Andy Howorth   Steel Rigg © Northern Horizons

A 6-day itinerary starting in Newcastle upon Tyne (4 walking days)

Northumberland is the more difficult section of the route so we have suggested two itineraries: a Grade A which is a little bit more demanding, or Grade B which takes things at a slightly more leisurely pace.

Grade A
Day 1: Arrive in Newcastle and explore this vibrant and historic city of the north.

Day 2: Take the Metro train to Wallsend and walk to Newburn (12 miles). Return to Newcastle by service bus for a second night there.

Day 3: Walk from Newburn to Chollerford (17 miles).

Day 4: Walk from Chollerford to Steel Rigg (12½ miles).

TRIP HIGHLIGHTS:
- Segedunum Roman Fort and Museum
- Newcastle's historic quayside and bridges
- Bessie Surtees' House (English Heritage – free)
- Great North Museum
- Grainger Town and Grey Street: "the loveliest street in England"
- Housesteads, Chesters and Vindolanda Roman Forts
- Hadrian's Wall, its Forts, Milecastles, Turrets, Vallum and Wall-ditch
- Metro Centre (shopping, eating, entertainment)
- BALTIC Centre for Contemporary Art
- The Sage Gateshead
- The Biscuit Factory – contemporary art gallery

Day 5: Steel Rigg to Gilsland (9 miles). Stay in Gilsland or take the AD122 Hadrian's Wall Bus and train back to Newcastle for a final night in the city.

Day 6: Last-minute sight-seeing and souvenir shopping in Newcastle before returning home.

Grade B
Day 1: Arrive in Newcastle and explore this vibrant and historic city of the north.

Day 2: Take the Metro train to Wallsend and walk to Newcastle's Tyne bridges (6 miles).

Day 3: Catch the AD122 Hadrian's Wall Country Bus (or service bus) to Heddon-on-the-Wall and walk the National Trail to the Errington Arms on the A68 (10 miles); then take the AD122 Bus to Corbridge and visit Corbridge Roman Site.

Day 4: Take the Hadrian's Wall Country Line railway from Corbridge to Hexham, then take the AD122 / 880 bus to Chollerford; walk to Housesteads (10 miles).

Day 5: Walk from Housesteads to Cawfields (6 miles) then take the AD122 Hadrian's Wall Bus back to Newcastle.

Day 6: Last-minute sight-seeing and souvenir shopping in Newcastle before returning home.

View from Gateshead Millennium Bridge © Andy Howorth

The Roman Ring

An alternative long distance route that explores
Hadrian's Wall Country

HADRIAN'S WALL
COUNTRY

The Roman Ring, combined with the
Moss Troopers' Trail and Hadrian's
Wall Path, opens up new and exciting
walking possibilities and opportunities
within the broad central sector of
Hadrian's Wall Country between
Brampton and Corbridge. The Roman
Ring guidebook reveals a network of
routes enabling walkers to explore
the diversity and richness of the
landscape.

*The Roman Ring guidebook by Mark Richards is available
to purchase from the Hadrian's Wall Country Online Shop
www.hadrians-wall.org*

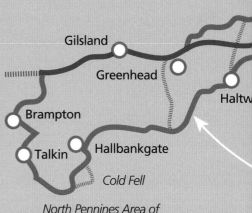

Moss Troopers' Trail
Carvoran to Newbrough
32 km / 20 miles > 2 days

Northu⟨
Nationa⟨

Gilsland

Greenhead

Haltw⟨

Brampton

Talkin Hallbankgate

Cold Fell

*North Pennines Area of
Outstanding Natural Beauty*

Blood Stone at Cragend © Mark Richards

Haresby Lonnen © Mark Richards

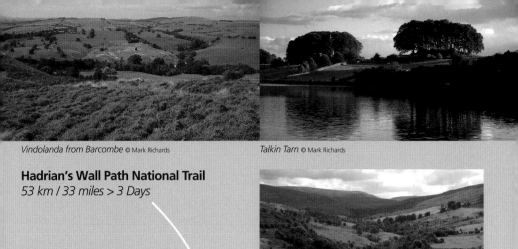

Vindolanda from Barcombe © Mark Richards

Talkin Tarn © Mark Richards

Hadrian's Wall Path National Trail
53 km / 33 miles > 3 Days

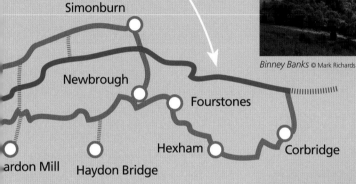

Binney Banks © Mark Richards

Simonburn

Newbrough

Fourstones

Hexham

Corbridge

ardon Mill   Haydon Bridge

The Roman Ring
Haytongate to Halton Chesters
83 km / 52 miles > 4 days

The Moot Hall, Hexham © Mark Richards

Tindale Fell Cairn © Mark Richards

North Sea

Tynemouth

Priory

North Shields

Fish Quays

Ferry Port

Ferry Port Customs House

Marina

Tynemouth M

North Shields M

Tynemouth

B1344

B1344

ARBEIA

South Shields

South Shields Museum

M Chichester

M Tyne Dock

A1018

A1300

A194

Catherine Cookson's birthplace

Simonside

A185

Bede

Bede's World

Jarrow

A19

Meadowell M

Percy Main

A187

A193

Royal Quays Outlet Centre

River Tyne

Tyne Tunnel

Tyne Tunnel Pedestrian Access

Howdon

A193

A187

Jarrow M

A185

Hebburn

A1058

A19

Hadrian Road

Wallsend M

Wallsend

SEGEDUNUM

Key

- Main Walk (Hadrian's Cycleway Route 72)
- Alternative
- National Trail
- **P** Parking
- **M** Metro
- Refreshments
- Beach
- Start/finish National Trail
- Start point
- **i** Tourist Information Centre

12

hadrians-wall.org

Fort-to-Fort

Location:
North and South Tyneside

Linear walk

Directions
- Follow Route 72 Hadrian's Cycleway between Segedunum Roman Fort and Tynemouth Priory.

- Take the ferry between North and South Shields to visit Arbeia Roman Fort.

- Alternatively, use the pedestrian access for the Tyne Tunnel between Howden and Jarrow and follow NCN 72 & 14 to South Shields.

Distance
Up to 8 miles

Estimated walk time
3 – 4 hours plus visiting time

Grade
Easy

Suggested start/finish
Segedunum Roman Fort (Grid Ref: NZ 301 660)

Tourist information
North Shields Tourist Information Centre, Royal Quays
Tel: 0191 200 5895
South Shields, Museum & Art Gallery
Tel: 0191 456 8740

Public transport
Tyne and Wear Metro to Segedunum (Wallsend); Tynemouth and South Shields (combined Metro and ferry day tickets available); ferry terminal. Bus services on route.

Ordnance Survey map
Explorer sheet 316 Newcastle upon Tyne

Places to eat and drink
Café at Segedunum Roman Fort; plus several cafés and restaurants in Wallsend, Tynemouth South Shields and North Shields

Other walks in this area
Coastal walks from the amphitheatre on Sea Road at South Shields to Frenchman's Bay, Souter Light House and Marsden Rock. North Tyneside Waggonways (www.waggonways.co.uk)

Highlights
- Arbeia Roman Fort with reconstructed barracks and gatehouse (free entry)
- Catherine Cookson birthplace
- Customs House South Shields
- Historic fish quays
- Pedestrian tunnel under the Tyne
- Reconstructed section of Hadrian's Wall at Segedunum
- Segedunum Roman Fort and Museum with reconstructed bath house
- Tynemouth Priory (English Heritage)

Segedunum Roman Fort

Arbeia Roman Fort

© Tyne and Wear Museums

© Tyne and Wear Museums

Nearby attractions
- Bede's World
- Blue Reef Aquarium
- Childhood Memories Toy Museum (Tynemouth)
- Royal Quays (shopping outlet)
- Royal Quays Marina
- Seaton Delaval Hall (National Trust)
- South Shields Museum and Art Gallery
- Stephenson Railway Museum
- St Paul's Monastery (Jarrow)
- Tynemouth / South Shields beaches
- Tynemouth Priory (English Heritage)
- Souter Lighthouse (National Trust)
- Wet 'n' Wild (North Shields)
- Whitley Bay Ice Rink

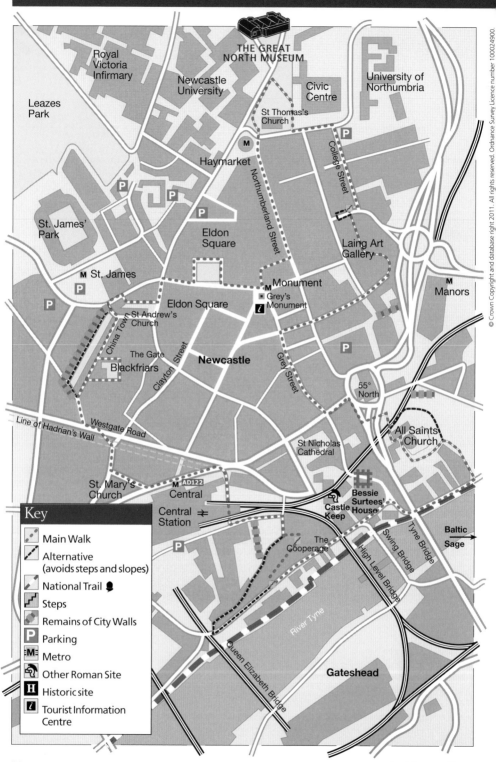

THE GREAT NORTH MUSEUM

Royal Victoria Infirmary

Newcastle University

Civic Centre

University of Northumbria

Leazes Park

St Thomas's Church

M Haymarket

College Street

St. James' Park

Eldon Square

Laing Art Gallery

M St. James

P

Monument

M Grey's Monument

M Manors

Eldon Square

St Andrew's Church

China Town

The Gate

Clayton Street

Newcastle

Grey Street

P

Blackfriars

55° North

Line of Hadrian's Wall

Westgate Road

All Saints Church

St Nicholas Cathedral

St. Mary's Church

M AD122 Central

Central Station

The Cooperage

Castle Keep

Bessie Surtees' House

Baltic Sage →

P

High Level Bridge

Swing Bridge

Tyne Bridge

River Tyne

Queen Elizabeth Bridge

Gateshead

Key

	Main Walk
	Alternative (avoids steps and slopes)
	National Trail
	Steps
	Remains of City Walls
P	Parking
M	Metro
	Other Roman Site
H	Historic site
i	Tourist Information Centre

hadrians-wall.org

Around the Medieval Town Walls

Location:

Newcastle City

Directions
● Work your way around the route starting at any point.

Highlights
- 17th century Bessie Surtees' House (English Heritage – free entry)
- Chinatown
- Medieval town wall and streets (medieval street map available at www.nationaltrail.co.uk /hadrianswall (Planning a Trip))
- Georgian planned town
- Grey Street, the "loveliest street in England"
- Newcastle quayside
- Norman keep, on the site of the original Roman fort (Pons Aelius)

Castle Keep

© NewcastleGateshead Initiative

Circular walk

Distance
3 miles

Estimated walk time
1½ hours plus browsing and visiting time

Grade
Easy

Suggested start/finish
Bessie Surtees' House
(Grid Ref: NZ 251 638)

Tourist information
Central Arcade, Tourist Information Centre, Newcastle City Centre
Tel: 0191 277 8000

Public transport
Haymarket, Monument and Central Station Metros; Quaylink bus services (linking bus, Metro and train services), AD122 Hadrian's Wall Country Bus, Central Station

Ordnance Survey map
Explorer sheet 316 Newcastle upon Tyne

Places to eat and drink
Newcastle has many cafés, pubs and restaurants

Other walks in this area
www.newcastlegateshead. com/walkingguides

Nearby attractions
- BALTIC Centre for Contemporary Art
- Biscuit Factory – contemporary art gallery
- Denton Hall Turret and West Denton Hadrian's Wall
- Discovery Museum
- Eldon Square Shopping Centre
- Great North Museum
- Hatton Gallery
- Laing Art Gallery
- Saltwell Park and Towers (Gateshead)
- Seven Stories, The Centre for Children's Books
- Shipley Art Gallery (Gateshead)
- The Sage Gateshead
- Theatre Royal
- Tyne Bridges

Bessie Surtees' House

© English Heritage

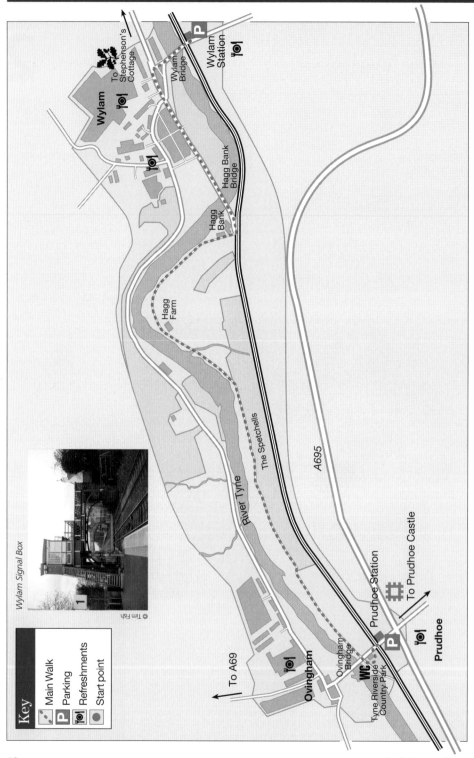

Wylam Signal Box

© Tim Fish

Key
- Main Walk
- **P** Parking
- Refreshments
- Start point

Wylam

To Stephenson's Cottage

Wylam Bridge

Wylam Station

Hagg Bank Bridge

Hagg Bank

Hagg Farm

River Tyne

The Spetchells

A695

Prudhoe Station

To Prudhoe Castle

Prudhoe

Ovingham

Ovingham Bridge

WC

Tyne Riverside Country Park

To A69

hadrians-wall.org

Wylam to Prudhoe

Location:
Alongside the River Tyne

Directions

● From Wylam walk along the Wylam Wagonway, signed for Newburn; Stephenson's Cottage is ½ mile away.

● Re-trace your steps back to Wylam and remain on the footpath to Prudhoe, crossing Hagg Bank bridge (one of the first bowed-arched bridges to be built anywhere in the world).

● Visit Prudhoe Castle and return to Wylam using the Tyne Valley railway line.

Highlights
- George Stephenson's Cottage (National Trust)
- Historic bowed-arched railway bridge at Wylam
- Prudhoe's Norman castle (English Heritage)
- Riverside walks
- World's oldest working railway station at Wylam

Prudhoe Castle

© English Heritage

Nearby attractions
- Cherryburn: Thomas Bewick Birthplace (National Trust)
- Corbridge market town
- Corbridge Roman Site (Corstopitum) (English Heritage)
- Dilston Physic Garden Ltd
- Fifiefofum Fine Art Gallery (Newton)
- Gibside (National Trust)
- Hadrian's Wall at Heddon-on-the-Wall
- Hexham Abbey
- Hexham Old Gaol
- Ryton Willows
- Tyne Riverside Country Park
- Wylam Railway Station

Linear walk

Distance
3½ miles

Estimated walk time
2½ hours plus visiting time

Grade
Easy

Suggested start/finish
Wylam car park
(Grid Ref: NZ 120 646)

Tourist information
Tourist Information point at Prudhoe Waterworld
Tel: 01661 833144

Public transport
Hadrian's Wall Country Line, Wylam and Prudhoe railway stations; 684 bus service, Newcastle-Throckley-Ovington/Hexham

Ordnance Survey map
Explorer sheet 316
Newcastle upon Tyne

Places to eat and drink
Wylam has plenty of cafés, restaurants and pubs, including a micro brewery

Other walks in this area
Tyne Valley Train Trails linking Wylam with Prudhoe, Stocksfield, Riding Mill, Corbridge and Hexham railway stations, Derwent Walk (Consett). (Enquire at Tourist Information Centre)

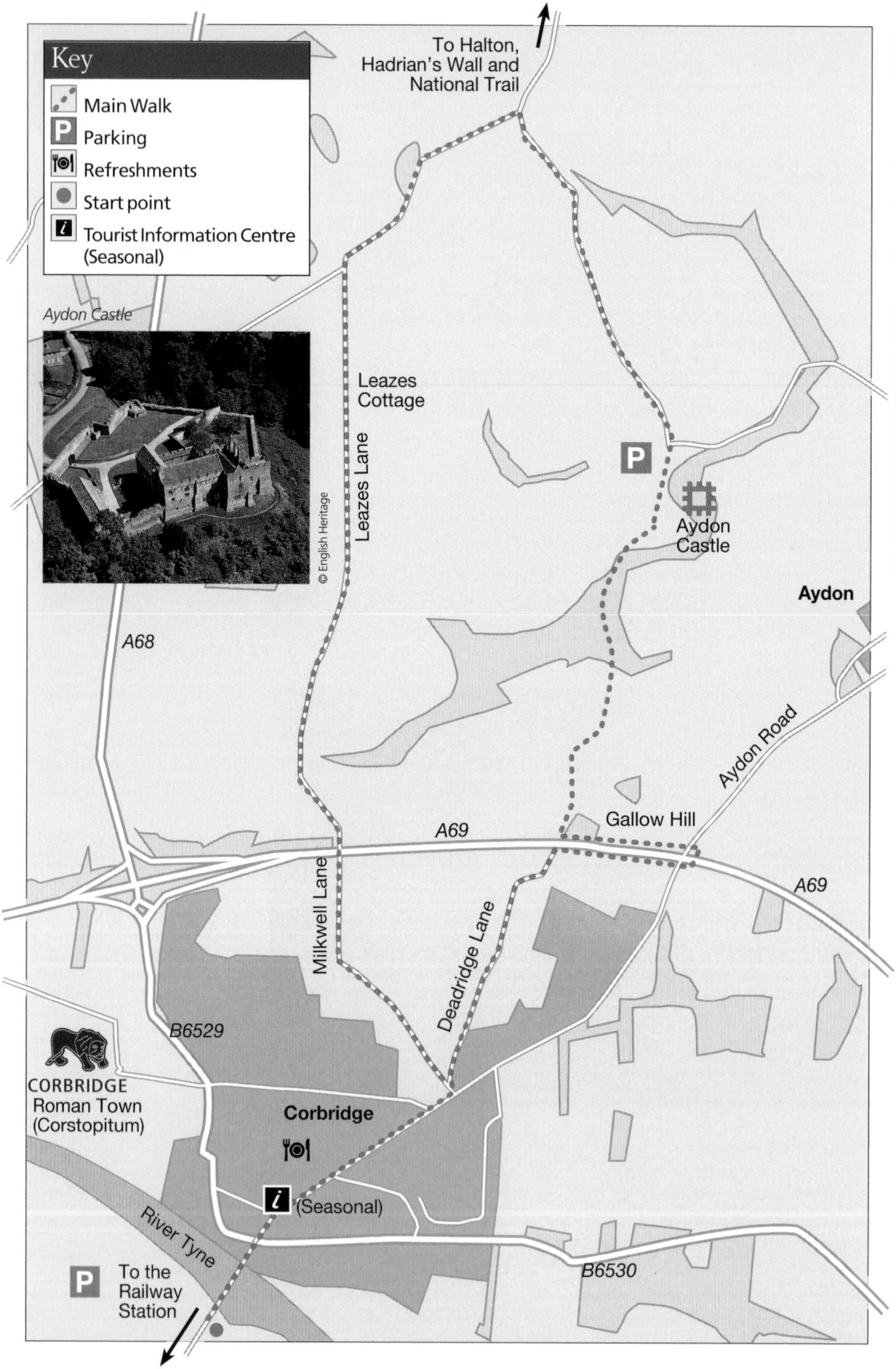

Key

- Main Walk
- **P** Parking
- **[O]** Refreshments
- ● Start point
- **[i]** Tourist Information Centre (Seasonal)

Aydon Castle

© English Heritage

To Halton,
Hadrian's Wall and
National Trail

Leazes
Cottage

Leazes Lane

P

Aydon
Castle

Aydon

A68

Aydon Road

A69

Gallow Hill

A69

Milkwell Lane

Deadridge Lane

B6529

CORBRIDGE
Roman Town
(Corstopitum)

Corbridge

[O]

[i] (Seasonal)

River Tyne

P To the
Railway
Station

B6530

hadrians-wall.org

Corbridge and Aydon Castle

Location:

Corbridge, Northumberland

Circular walk

Distance
6 miles

Estimated walk time
4 to 5 hours plus visiting time

Grade
Moderate

Directions

● Head across the river into Princes Street, which becomes Aydon Road.

● Turn left by large gates (Riversdale) and immediately right into Deadridge Lane, signed bridleway to Aydon Castle, 1½ miles.

● At the lane end bear right (east) alongside the A69, crossing it at road bridge. Immediately follow the sign for Aydon Castle, follow path west along A69.

● After approximately ½ mile turn right, then follow waymarks across fields through a gate into woodland, the path rising steeply to Aydon Castle.

● After your visit turn right out of castle and follow the road. At car park continue ahead ignoring the road on your right. Stay on this road ignoring other minor roads that join from the right.

● After approximately 2 miles turn first left and carry straight on down Leazes Lane towards Corbridge, crossing the footbridge next to the ford, going under the A69 to visit pottery kilns on your right. Re-joining Aydon Road continue back into Corbridge.

Suggested start/finish
Corbridge car park, on the south side of the River Tyne. (Grid Ref: NY 988 640)

Tourist information
Corbridge Tourist Information Centre, Tel: 01434 632815
Hexham Tourist Information Centre, Tel: 01434 652220

Public transport
Hadrian's Wall Country railway line connects Corbridge to Carlisle and Newcastle; AD122 Hadrian's Wall Country Bus (between Easter and October); Route 10 bus to Hexham and Newcastle; 685 bus to Carlisle and Newcastle

Ordnance Survey map
Explorer (OL) 43 Hadrian's Wall and Explorer Sheet 316 Newcastle upon Tyne

Places to eat and drink
Many cafés, tea shops and pubs in Corbridge town centre.

Other walks in this area
Tyne Valley Train Trails linking Corbridge with Hexham, Haydon Bridge, Bardon Mill and Haltwhistle railway stations. (Enquire at Tourist Information Centre)

Highlights

• Ancient town of Corbridge
• Medieval Aydon Castle
(English Heritage)

• Corbridge Roman Town and Museum (Corstopitum)
(English Heritage)

Re-enactment at Corbridge

© Janine Howorth

Corbridge Roman Town

© English Heritage

Nearby attractions

• Brocksbushes Farm Shop
• Dilston Castle
• Dilston Physic Garden Ltd
• Fifiefofum Fine Art Gallery
(Newton)

• Hexham Abbey
• Hexham Moot Hall
• Hexham Old Gaol
• Queen's Hall, Hexham
• Tyne Green Country Park

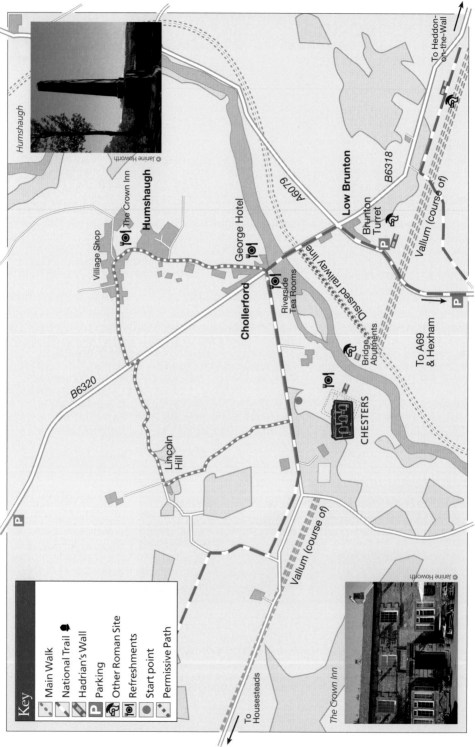

Key

- Main Walk
- National Trail
- Hadrian's Wall
- P Parking
- Other Roman Site
- Refreshments
- Start point
- Permissive Path

Humshaugh

© Janine Howorth

The Crown Inn

Village Shop

Humshaugh

George Hotel

Chollerford

Riverside Tea Rooms

B6320

Lincoln Hill

A6079

Disused railway line

Low Brunton

Brunton Turret

B6318

Vallum (course of)

To Heddon-on-the-Wall

Bridge Abutments

To A69 & Hexham

CHESTERS

Vallum (course of)

To Housesteads

The Crown Inn

© Janine Howorth

hadrians-wall.org

Chesters and Humshaugh

Location:
Chesters Roman Fort

Directions
● From Chesters Roman Fort walk up the quiet lane and turn right to Lincoln Hill.

● You will arrive at a crossroads, turn right here, this part of the route will be signed for the Cycle Byway.

● After about ½ mile, cross the main road and continue into Humshaugh.

● Admire the magnificent eastward views from the war memorial, and walk through the village.

● Leaving the village follow the road back to Chollerford and Chesters Roman Fort.

Highlights
● Chesters Roman Fort
(English Heritage)

● Humshaugh village and church

Chesters Roman Fort

© English Heritage

Distance
2½ miles

Estimated walk time
1 hour walking plus time to visit attractions

Grade
Easy

Suggested start/finish
Chesters Roman Fort
(Grid Ref: NY 910 704)

Tourist information
Hexham Tourist Information Centre,
Tel: 01434 652220

Public transport
AD122 Hadrian's Wall Country Bus 9 (Easter to October), 880 all year to Chollerford

Ordnance Survey map
Explorer (OL) 43 Hadrian's Wall

Places to eat and drink
Crown Inn, Humshaugh; George Hotel and Riverside tea room at Chollerford; "Lucullus's Larder" at Chesters Roman Fort (site visitors only)

Other walks in this area
Walks Around the Mid-Tyne (Wall, Humshaugh and Chollerford). (Enquire at Tourist Information Centre)

Nearby attractions
● Brocolitia Fort and the Temple of Mithras
● Brunton Turret
● Chesters Bridge abutment
● Chesters Walled Garden
● Hadrian's Wall

● Hexham Abbey
● Hexham Moot Hall and Gallery
● Hexham Queen's Hall
● Housesteads Roman Fort
   (English Heritage / National Trust)
● Roman Vindolanda

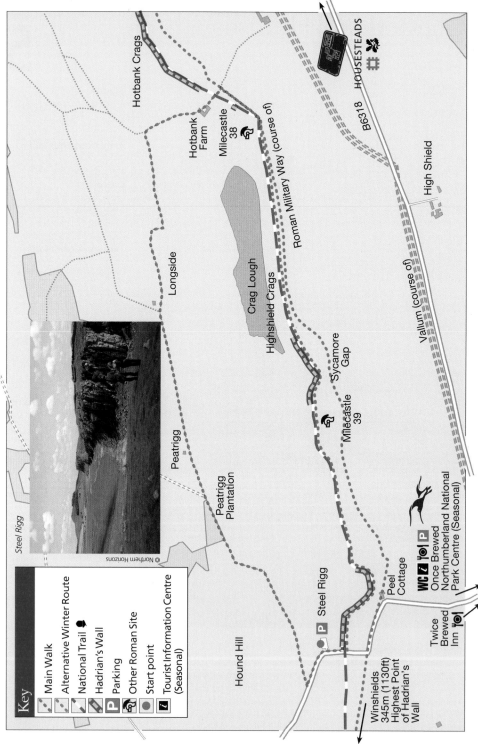

Key

- Main Walk
- Alternative Winter Route
- National Trail
- Hadrian's Wall
- Parking **P**
- Other Roman Site
- Start point
- Tourist Information Centre (Seasonal) **i**

© Northern Horizons

Steel Rigg

Hound Hill

Peatrigg

Peatrigg Plantation

Hotbank Crags

Longside

Hotbank Farm

Milecastle 38

Crag Lough

Highshield Crags

Roman Military Way (course of)

Sycamore Gap

Milecastle 39

HOUSESTEADS

B6318

High Shield

Vallum (course of)

Steel Rigg **P**

P Steel Rigg

Winshields 345m (1130ft) Highest Point of Hadrian's Wall

Peel Cottage

WC **i** **P** Once Brewed Northumberland National Park Centre (Seasonal)

Twice Brewed Inn

hadrians-wall.org

A "barbarian" view of the Wall

Location:
Hadrian's Wall in Northumberland National Park

Directions
● Turn right out of Steel Rigg car park and in a couple of hundred yards bear right along a track signed "footpath to Hotbank 1½ miles", towards first Peatrigg plantation, then the buildings of Peatrigg and Longside.

● Continue east and soon after crossing a second footbridge take the path signed to the right towards Hotbank farm.

● Emerge onto Hadrian's Wall Path National Trail at the earthwork remains of Milecastle 38. Turn right and follow the National Trail Acorn waymarks back towards Steel Rigg.

Highlights
- Hadrian's Wall
- Landscape panoramas
- Steel Rigg
- Sycamore Gap

- The barbarian view of the Wall, from the north
- The Whin Sill

Sycamore Gap

© HWHU / Northern Horizons

Nearby attractions
- Brocolitia Fort and the Temple of Mithras
- Cawfield Crags
- Chesters Roman Fort
  (English Heritage)
- Hexham market town
- Housesteads Roman Fort
  (English Heritage / National Trust)
- Northumberland National Park Centre, Once Brewed

- Pennine Way National Trail
- Roman Army Museum (Carvoran)
- Roman Vindolanda
- Walltown Crags
- Whinshields highest point on Hadrian's Wall 345 metres (1,132 ft)

Circular walk

Distance
3½ miles

Estimated walk time
2+ hours

Grade
Strenuous (several steep slopes)

Suggested start/finish
Steel Rigg car park (Grid Ref: NY 751 677)

Tourist information
Once Brewed Visitor Centre Tel: 01434 344396

Public transport
AD122 Hadrian's Wall Country Bus (between Easter and October)

Ordnance Survey map
Explorer (OL) 43 Hadrian's Wall

Places to eat and drink
Twice Brewed Inn; Milecastle Inn

Other walks in this area
"A Walk in the Park". A selection of ten guided walks. Information from the Once Brewed Visitor Centre or visit www.northumberland nationalpark.org.uk

CONSERVATION TIP:
November to April when ground conditions are wet return to Steel Rigg along the footpath signed the Roman Military Way.

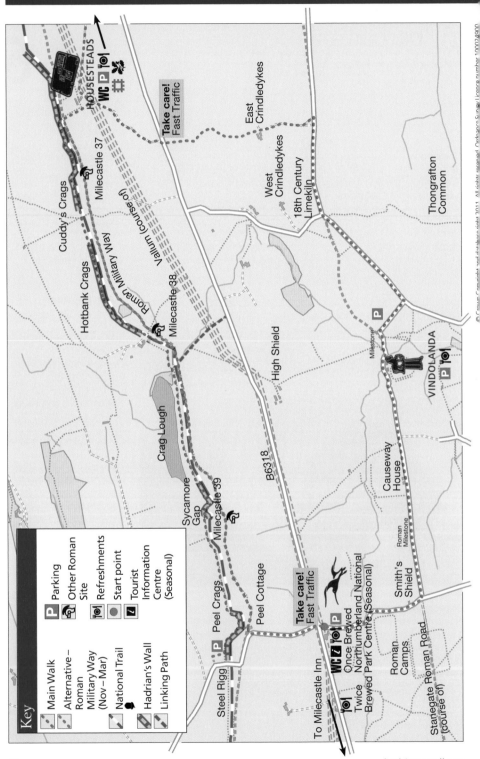

Key

Main Walk	Parking		
Alternative – Roman Military Way (Nov – Mar)	Other Roman Site		
National Trail	Refreshments		
Hadrian's Wall	Start point		
Linking Path	Tourist Information Centre (Seasonal)		

HOUSESTEADS
WC P

Take care!
Fast Traffic

East Crindledykes

Milecastle 37

Cuddy's Crags

West Crindledykes

18th Century Limekiln

Thongrafton Common

Hotbank Crags

Roman Military Way

Vallum (course of)

Milecastle 38

High Shield

Milestone

VINDOLANDA
P

Crag Lough

Sycamore Gap

Milecastle 39

B6318

Causeway House

Peel Crags

Peel Cottage

Smith's Shield

Roman Milestone

Take care!
Fast Traffic

Steel Rigg
P

Once Brewed
Twice Brewed
Northumberland National
Brewed Park Centre (Seasonal)

WC i P

Roman Camps

Stanegate Roman Road (course of)

To Milecastle Inn

hadrians-wall.org

Once Brewed, Roman Vindolanda and Housesteads

Location:
Hadrian's Wall in Northumberland National Park

Directions
● Leaving the Northumberland National Park Centre, Once Brewed, cross the B6318 (taking care) at the dog-leg junction signed for Steel Rigg.

● Before reaching Steel Rigg car park join Hadrian's Wall Path National Trail via the gate signed for Housesteads. Follow the path in an easterly direction to Housesteads Roman Fort and Museum, a visit is highly recommended.

● From the Fort and Museum, follow the tarmac road in a south westerly direction from the old farmhouse down to the B6318

Military Road. Turn right and in only a few yards cross the road (taking care) to take the ladder stile signed for Crindledykes.

● After ¾ mile turn right onto a road (it is also the Roman Stanegate).

● Take the second road on the right for Roman Vindolanda. Once again, a visit is highly recommended, otherwise continue on the single track road around the back of the site and back onto the Stanegate.

● Turn right at the junction signed for Northumberland National Park Centre.

Housesteads Fort

© Northern Horizons

Vindolanda and Stanegate

© English Heritage

Circular walk

Distance
Up to 7½ miles

Estimated walk time
4 to 4½ hours plus browsing time

Grade
Strenuous (several steep slopes)

Suggested start/finish
Once Brewed Visitor Centre (Grid Ref: NY 752 669)

Tourist information
Once Brewed Visitor Centre Tel: 01434 344396

Public transport
AD122 Hadrian's Wall Country Bus (between Easter and October) stops at Once Brewed Visitor Centre, Housesteads and Roman Vindolanda

Ordnance Survey map
Explorer (OL) 43 Hadrian's Wall

Places to eat and drink
Once Brewed Visitor Centre; Twice Brewed Inn; refreshment kiosk at Housesteads car park; café at Roman Vindolanda (site visitors only); Milecastle Inn

Other walks in this area
Bardon Mill and Thorngrafton Common.

CONSERVATION TIP:
November to April when ground conditions are wet, walk between Steel Rigg and Housesteads on signed Roman Military Way.

Highlights
● Hadrian's Wall – spectacular section
● Housesteads Roman Fort (English Heritage/National Trust)
● Roman Military Way
● Stanegate Roman Road
● Roman Vindolanda
● Northumberland National Park Centre, Once Brewed

Nearby attractions
● Brocolitia Fort and the Temple of Mithras
● Cawfield Crags
● Chesters Roman Fort (English Heritage)
● Hexham market town
● Pennine Way National Trail
● Roman Army Museum (Carvoran)
● Walltown Crags

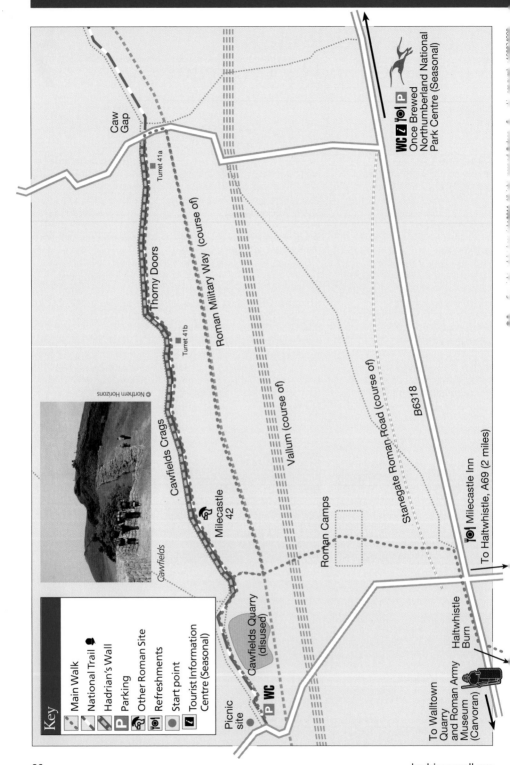

Key

- Main Walk
- National Trail
- Hadrian's Wall
- P Parking
- Other Roman Site
- Refreshments
- Start point
- Tourist Information Centre (Seasonal)

Caw Gap

Turret 41a

Thorny Doors

Turret 41b

Roman Military Way (course of)

© Northern Horizons

Cawfields Crags

Cawfields

Milecastle 42

Vallum (course of)

Cawfields Quarry (disused)

Roman Camps

Picnic site

P WC

Stanegate Roman Road (course of)

B6318

WC Z ⦿ P Once Brewed Northumberland National Park Centre (Seasonal)

⦿ Milecastle Inn

To Haltwhistle, A69 (2 miles)

To Walltown Quarry and Roman Army Museum (Carvoran)

Haltwhistle Burn

hadrians-wall.org

Cawfields to Caw Gap

Location:
Hadrian's Wall in Northumberland National Park

Directions
● From Cawfields Quarry car park walk east past the quarry lake towards Milecastle 42.

● With Hadrian's Wall on your left, follow the National Trail as far as the road at Caw Gap.

● Turn immediately to your right, in a few yards cross over the stile signed Cawfields Quarry 1 mile.

● Follow the low-level route next to the Vallum and Roman Military Way back to Cawfields Quarry.

Highlights
- 2 National Trails (Hadrian's Wall Path and Pennine Way)
- Cawfields Quarry
- Hadrian's Wall
- Milecastle 42
- Roman Military Way
- Turret 41a (Caw Gap)
- Turret 41b (Thorny Doors)
- Vallum – the bank and ditch earthwork
- Whin Sill

Cawfields

© Northern Horizons

Nearby attractions
- Brocolitia Fort and the Temple of Mithras
- Cawfield Crags
- Chesters Roman Fort (English Heritage)
- Haltwhistle ('Centre of Britain')
- Hexham market town
- Housesteads Roman Fort (English Heritage/National Trust)
- Roman Army Museum (Carvoran)
- Roman Vindolanda
- Thirlwall Castle
- Walltown Quarry
- Willowford Roman bridge abutment
- Northumberland National Park Centre, Once Brewed
- Pennine Way National Trail

Circular walk

Distance
2 miles

Estimated walk time
1 hour

Grade
Moderate (some steep slopes)

Suggested start/finish
Cawfields Quarry car park (Grid Ref: NY 714 666)

Tourist information
Once Brewed Visitor Centre Tel: 01434 344396

Public transport
AD122 Hadrian's Wall Country Bus (between Easter and October)

Ordnance Survey map
Explorer (OL) 43 Hadrian's Wall

Places to eat and drink
Milecastle Inn ½ mile on B6318 military road; picnic table at Cawfields Quarry; Haltwhistle, Herding Hill Farm Shop and cafe

Other walks in this area
Greenhead and Blenkinsopp Common (includes Walltown Quarry). (Enquire at Tourist Information Centre)

CONSERVATION TIP:
November to April when ground conditions are wet, help protect underlying archaeology next to the Wall by using the Military Way.

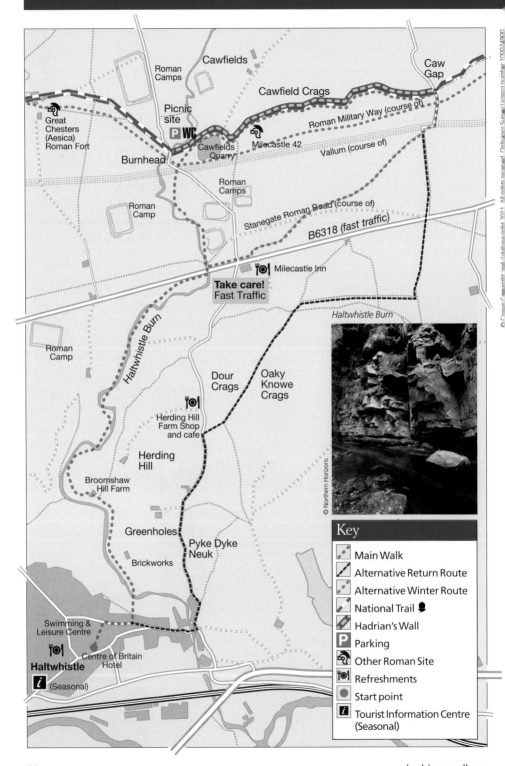

Cawfields

Caw Gap

Roman Camps

Cawfield Crags

Great Chesters (Aesica) Roman Fort

Picnic site

Roman Military Way (course of)

P **WC**

Burnhead

Cawfields Quarry

Milecastle 42

Vallum (course of)

Roman Camps

Roman Camp

Stanegate Roman Road (course of)

B6318 (fast traffic)

Milecastle Inn

Take care! Fast Traffic

Roman Camp

Haltwhistle Burn

Dour Crags

Oaky Knowe Crags

Herding Hill Farm Shop and cafe

© Northern Horizons

Herding Hill

Broomshaw Hill Farm

Greenholes

Pyke Dyke Neuk

Brickworks

Swimming & Leisure Centre

Centre of Britain Hotel

Haltwhistle

i (Seasonal)

Key	
	Main Walk
	Alternative Return Route
	Alternative Winter Route
	National Trail **🛡**
	Hadrian's Wall
P	Parking
	Other Roman Site
🍴	Refreshments
●	Start point
i	Tourist Information Centre (Seasonal)

Haltwhistle Burn to Cawfields

Location:
Haltwhistle is on the edge of Northumberland National Park

Directions

● From the 'Centre of Britain' sign walk through the archway opposite and into the supermarket car park.

● Turn right out of car park entrance uphill for 200 yards to Fairfield housing estate.

● Take immediate left after Fairfield marked to Haltwhistle Burn (sign fixed to wall).

● Go through metal kissing gate, passing playing field to reach a second gate.

● Descend steps to footbridge and follow burn-side path to old brickworks.

● Continue until you reach the military road, turning right (take care when crossing road), then soon after follow the path signed for Cawfields.

● From Cawfields Quarry car park follow Hadrian's Wall Path National Trail east for 1 mile.

● At Caw Gap turn right along the road and take the second footpath, signed for Milecastle Inn ½ mile.

● Re-trace your steps to Haltwhistle Burn and then return to Haltwhistle.

Highlights
- Haltwhistle ('Centre of Britain')
- Whin Sill
- Hadrian's Wall
- Industrial archaeology – lime kilns, brickworks
- "Lovers' Walk" river valley (Haltwhistle Ring Walk No. 3)

Circular walk

Distance
6 miles

Estimated walk time
4 to 5 hours plus browsing time

Grade
Strenuous (with some steep slopes)

Suggested start/finish
Centre of Britain sign (Grid Ref: NY 707 641)

Tourist information
Haltwhistle Tourist Information Centre
Tel: 01434 322002

Public transport
AD122 Hadrian's Wall Country Bus (Easter to October), 185 and 685 buses; Hadrian's Wall Country Railway Line

Ordnance Survey map
Explorer (OL) 43 Hadrian's Wall

Places to eat and drink
Milecastle Inn; Herding Hill Farm Shop and cafe plus cafés, hotels and pubs in Haltwhistle

Other walks in this area
A series of 20+ walks known as the Haltwhistle Rings (details from Haltwhistle Tourist Information Centre or visit www.haltwhistle.org)

Haltwhistle Burn
© Northern Horizons

Cawfields
© Northern Horizons

CONSERVATION TIP: November to April when ground conditions are wet, use the Military Way between Cawfields and Caw Gap.

Nearby attractions
- Chesters Roman Fort (English Heritage)
- Hexham market town
- Housesteads Roman Fort (English Heritage/National Trust)
- Once Brewed National Park Visitor Centre
- Pennine Way National Trail
- Roman Army Museum (Carvoran)
- Roman Vindolanda
- Walltown Crags
- Willowford Roman bridge abutment

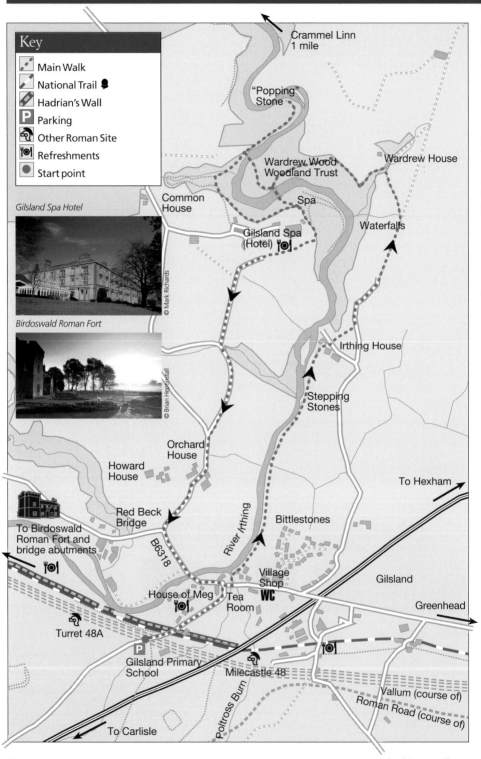

Key
- Main Walk
- National Trail
- Hadrian's Wall
- P Parking
- Other Roman Site
- Refreshments
- Start point

Gilsland Spa Hotel

Birdoswald Roman Fort

© Mark Richards

© Brian Hephistall

Crammel Linn
1 mile

"Popping"
Stone

Wardrew Wood
Woodland Trust

Wardrew House

Common
House

Spa

Gilsland Spa
(Hotel)

Waterfalls

Irthing House

Stepping
Stones

Orchard
House

Howard
House

To Hexham

Red Beck
Bridge

Bittlestones

To Birdoswald
Roman Fort and
bridge abutments

River Irthing

B6318

Village
Shop

Gilsland

WC

House of Meg

Tea
Room

Greenhead

Turret 48A

Gilsland Primary
School

P

Milecastle 48

Vallum (course of)

Roman Road (course of)

To Carlisle

Poltross Burn

30

hadrians-wall.org

Gilsland Spa *"Popping-stone"* and Birdoswald

Location:
Cumbria/Northumberland borders

Directions

● Turn right out of the car park towards the village centre, passing the House of Meg tea room.

● Turn right, crossing the bridge, and almost immediately take the footpath on the left signed for Irthing House ½ mile.

● At Irthing House walk ahead and go through a wicket gate followed by two stiles to a minor road.

● Turn left and in a quarter of a mile take the drive on the left signed for Wardrew House.

● Take the first path left, to enter the Woodland Trust's Irthing Gorge wood.

● Shortly pass a footbridge on the left, an optional short-cut to the Gilsland Spa hotel.

● At second footbridge, cross River Irthing. Turn right, walk to

Sir Walter Scott's "Popping-stone" (path often muddy), where he is said to have proposed to his wife; re-trace your steps back to the footbridge.

● Do not re-cross the bridge but stay on the main path, ignoring linking paths joining from the right, to the Gilsland Spa hotel. Walk around the hotel and along its driveway down to the road and back into Gilsland.

● Back at the car park you now have the option of walking 1¼ miles to Birdoswald Roman Fort (English Heritage). Follow the brown sign indicating Willowford ½ mile and cross the River Irthing over the National Trail's award winning footbridge.

● You can either re-trace your steps back to Gilsland or return using the AD122 Hadrian's Wall Bus.

Circular walk

Distance
3½ miles (+ optional 2½ miles to Birdoswald Roman Fort)

Estimated walk time
2½ hours plus browsing time

Grade
Moderate

Suggested start/finish
Gilsland car park, next to village primary school (Grid Ref: NY 631 662)

Tourist information
Haltwhistle Tourist Information Centre
Tel: 01434 322002

Public transport
AD122 Hadrian's Wall Country Bus (between Easter and October); Hadrian's Wall Country Railway Line

Ordnance Survey map
Explorer (OL) 43 Hadrian's Wall

Places to eat and drink
House of Meg tea room and pubs in Gilsland, Gilsland Spa Hotel, café at Birdoswald Roman Fort

Other walks in this area
From Gilsland to Birdoswald (see above directions). (Enquire at Tourist Information Centre)

Highlights
• River Irthing gorge
• Sir Walter Scott's "Popping-stone" where he proposed marriage to his wife
• Optional link to Birdoswald Roman Fort (English Heritage)
• Hadrian's Wall and Roman bridge abutments

Nearby attractions
• Bewcastle
• Birdoswald Roman Fort and Visitor Centre (English Heritage)
• Lanercost Priory (English Heritage)
• New Mills Trout Farm (Brampton)
• Talkin Tarn Country Park (Brampton)
• Once Brewed Northumberland National Park Centre
• Poltross Burn and Milecastle 48
• Roman Army Museum (Carvoran)
• Walltown Quarry
• Willowford Roman bridge abutment

Crammel Linn waterfall where the water has cut through the sandstone to give a 10m drop.

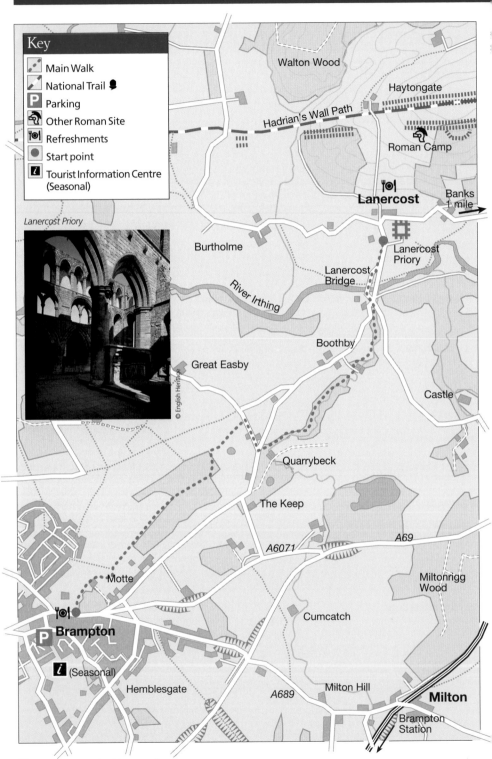

Key

- **Main Walk**
- **National Trail** 🚶
- **P** Parking
- 🐎 Other Roman Site
- 🍽 Refreshments
- ● Start point
- **ℹ** Tourist Information Centre (Seasonal)

Lanercost Priory

© English Heritage

Walton Wood

Haytongate

Hadrian's Wall Path

🐎 Roman Camp

🍽 **Lanercost**

Banks 1 mile →

Burtholme

Lanercost Priory

Lanercost Bridge

River Irthing

Boothby

Great Easby

Castle

Quarrybeck

The Keep

A69

A6071

Miltonrigg Wood

Motte

Cumcatch

🍽 **P** **Brampton**

ℹ (Seasonal)

Hemblesgate

A689

Milton Hill

Milton

Brampton Station

Brampton to Lanercost

Location:
Cumbria

Distance
4 miles

Estimated walk time
2½ hours

Grade
Easy

Suggested start/finish
Brampton Market Place
(Grid Ref: NY 531 612)

Tourist information
Moot Hall, Market Place,
Brampton
Tel: 016977 3433

Public transport
AD122 Hadrian's Wall
Country Bus (between
Easter and October)

Ordnance Survey map
Ordnance Survey Explorer
Map 315

Places to eat and drink
Off the Wall Tearoom
(Brampton) and Lanercost
Tearoom & Art Gallery

Other walks in this area
Many walks around
Brampton and the River
Irthing.

Directions

● From the Market Place go to High Cross Street. At the main road junction go right, cross the zebra crossing and follow the footway passing the Brampton Playhouse and up the steps onto The Moat. A huge glacier left this long ridge behind as it melted. Saxons held their councils on a mound, "The Moat" which they constructed on the highest end of the ridge. At its centre is an imposing bronze statue of the 7th Earl of Carlisle from nearby Naworth Castle, who died in 1864.

● Descend into the lane running up the north side of the wooded hill. After a kissing-gate wander along the top of the pasture. Soon a metal kissing-gate right gives access into Ridgewood, the Woodland Trust land running along Brampton Ridge. Walk beside the row of beech trees, there are great views all along this section.

● Go through the squeeze stiles, and continue along the path. Follow way-marking down through a young coniferous planting to a kissing-gate. The path joins a bridleway, keep sharp right to a gate entering a green lane. Pass a well-sited seat, which gives a lovely view from Craggle Hill and Haytongate round by the distant hills of Christianbury Crags and the Liddlesdale hills to the table-topped Burnswark and Criffel to the west. The bridle-lane exits into a minor road, turn right rising over the brow to meet the Lanercost road.

● Directly opposite a metal kissing-gate draws the walk into the woodland passing on down to come by Quarrybeck Cottage and then along Quarry Beck. Go past the workshops be careful crossing the road and continue alongside the beck. Cross the footbridge to meet the Naworth road. Go left down the narrow hollow-way to arrive at the Lanercost road between the old corn mill and the former Abbey Bridge Hotel (both now B&Bs). Cross Abbey Bridge.

● Pass through the picnic area and walk along the road verge beyond the entrance to the tearoom car park to reach the kiosk and bus stop opposite the handsome stone gateway entrance to Lanercost Priory.

Banks Turrett, Hadrian's Wall

© HWHU / Heptinstall

Walk to Banks and along the National Trail towards Birdoswald Roman fort to experience Hadrian's Wall and the Irthing Valley

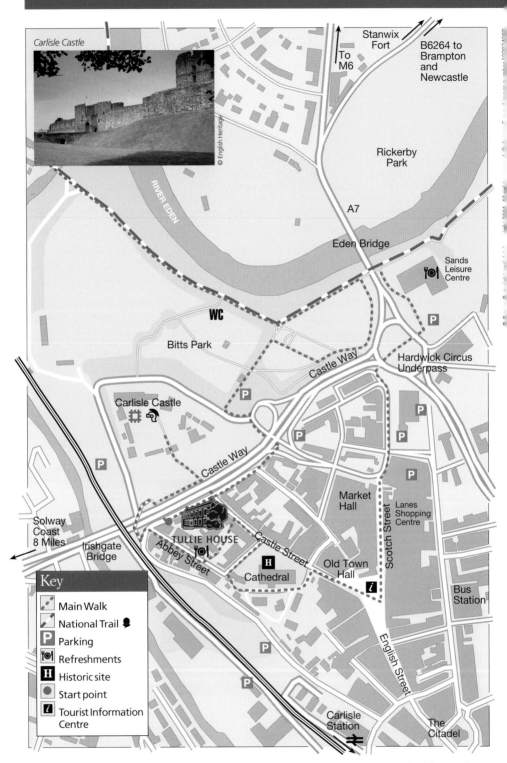

Carlisle Castle

© English Heritage

Stanwix Fort

To M6

B6264 to Brampton and Newcastle

RIVER EDEN

Rickerby Park

A7

Eden Bridge

Sands Leisure Centre

WC

Bitts Park

Castle Way

Hardwick Circus Underpass

Carlisle Castle

Castle Way

Solway Coast 8 Miles

Irishgate Bridge

TULLIE HOUSE

Abbey Street

Castle Street

Market Hall

Scotch Street

Lanes Shopping Centre

H Cathedral

Old Town Hall

i

Bus Station

English Street

Carlisle Station

The Citadel

Key

- Main Walk
- National Trail 🌳
- P Parking
- Refreshments
- H Historic site
- Start point
- i Tourist Information Centre

Historic Carlisle

Location:
Carlisle City's historic quarter

Directions
● Start the route from any point and follow it at your leisure.

Highlights
- Bitts Park
- Carlisle Castle (English Heritage) Luguvalium, the site of the roman fort at Carlisle, lies partly buried beneath the castle keep
- Carlisle Cathedral
- Carlisle Citadel
- Guildhall Museum
- Rickerby Park
- River Eden and riverside parkland
- Sands Leisure Centre
- The Lanes Shopping Centre
- Town Walls
- Tullie House Museum and Art Gallery

Tullie House

© Bryan Scott

Carlisle Cathedral

© Heptinstall

Nearby attractions
- Bewcastle Cross and Church
- Carlisle Racecourse
- Gretna Green (shopping outlet)
- Houghton Hall Garden Centre
- Lanercost Priory (English Heritage)
- New Mills Trout Farm (Brampton)
- Solway Aviation Museum (Carlisle Airport)
- Solway Coast Area of Outstanding Natural Beauty
- Stony Holme Golf Course
- Stanwix (Petrianum) Hadrian's Wall fort and settlement (Grid Ref: NY401571)
- Talkin Tarn Country Park (near Brampton)
- Walby Farm Park (Crosby)

Circular walk

Distance
1 ½ miles
Estimated walk time
1 hour for walk plus browsing and visiting time.
Grade
Easy
Suggested start/finish
Tullie House Museum and Art Gallery
(Grid Ref: NY 398 560)
Tourist information
Carlisle Tourist Information Centre Tel: 01228 625600
Public transport
Tyne Valley Railway Line to Newcastle;
Terminus of the Settle to Carlisle Railway;
AD122 Hadrian's Wall Country Bus (between Easter and October);
685 bus to Newcastle;
Local buses for Cumbria and southern Scotland
Ordnance Survey map
Explorer 315 Carlisle
Places to eat and drink
Carlisle Cathedral (Prior's Kitchen); Tullie House (Garden Restaurant); Sands Leisure Centre café; plus many other cafés, pubs and restaurants in Carlisle
Other walks in this area
Rickerby Park in Carlisle. (Enquire at Tourist Information Centre)

Tullie House Museum and Art Gallery – Roman Frontier Gallery, stories beyond Hadrian's Wall permanent exhibition

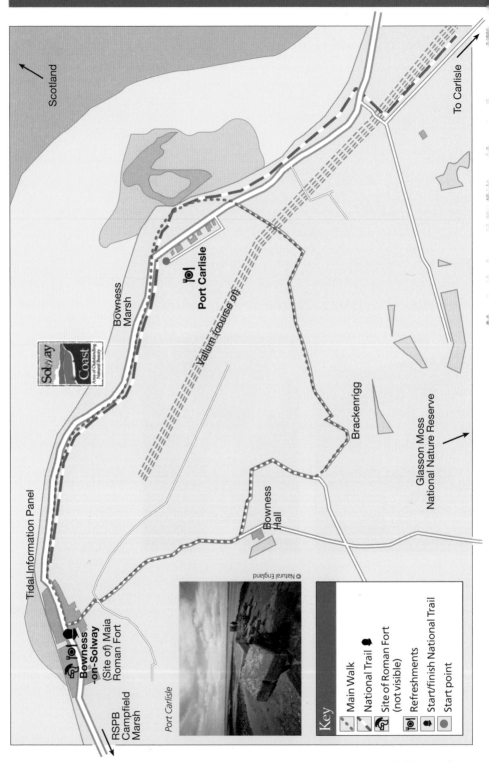

Scotland

To Carlisle

Bowness
Marsh

Port Carlisle

Vallum (course of)

Brackenrigg

Glasson Moss
National Nature Reserve

Bowness
Hall

© Natural England

Tidal Information Panel

Solway
Coast
Area of Outstanding
Natural Beauty

Bowness
-on-Solway
(Site of) Maia
Roman Fort

RSPB
Campfield
Marsh

Port Carlisle

Key

Main Walk

National Trail

Site of Roman Fort
(not visible)

Refreshments

Start/finish National Trail

Start point

36

hadrians-wall.org

Forts and Ports

13

Location:
Port Carlisle, Bowness-on-Solway in Solway Coast Area of Outstanding Natural Beauty

Directions
● From Port Carlisle follow the National Trail along the edge of the marsh into Bowness-on-Solway. Visit the Trail's start/finish point, signed the Banks Promenade.

● Turn left at the King's Arms pub following the road south. Pass Bowness Hall and after a mile take the footpath left, for Brackenrigg.

● After about a mile the path meets the main road beside the Methodist chapel. Cross the road and go through a gate onto a footpath that brings you back onto the Trail and into Port Carlisle.

Highlights
- Bird watching on Bowness Marsh
- Estuary views into Scotland
- Extensive panoramic views
- Haafnetting, the traditional
- Solway fishing practice in Bowness and Port Carlisle
- Port Carlisle's Historic Canal Basin
- RSPB Campfield Farm

Birdwatching, Bowness Marsh

Haaf Netters

© Rose Wolfe, Solway Coast AONB Unit

© Natural England / Charlie Hedley

Solway Firth

© Heptinstall

Nearby attractions
- Carlisle Castle (English Heritage)
- Carlisle Cathedral
- Drumburgh Moss NNR
- Edward I Memorial
- Glasson Moss NNR
- Solway Coast Discovery Centre
- Tullie House Museum and Art Gallery

Circular walk

Distance
3½ miles

Estimated walk time
2 hours

Grade
Moderate

Suggested start/finish
Hope and Anchor Inn, Port Carlisle
(Grid Ref: NY 240 621)

Tourist information
Solway Coast Discovery Centre, Silloth
Tel: 016973 31944

Public transport
Bus Service 93 (Carlisle to Bowness)

Ordnance Survey map
OS Explorer Map (314) Solway Firth, Wigton and Silloth

Places to eat and drink
Hope and Anchor Inn in Port Carlisle; King's Arms Inn and the Old Chapel tea room in Bowness

Other walks in this area
Solway Coastal Rambles (Bowness-on-Solway, Glasson, Drumburgh, Burgh by Sands, Beaumont). (Enquire at Tourist Information Centre)

SOLWAY TIDE TIMES
Bowness marsh is tidal and occasionally floods. Check at www.nationaltrail.co.uk/hadrianswall (Planning a Trip)

hadrians-wall.org

37

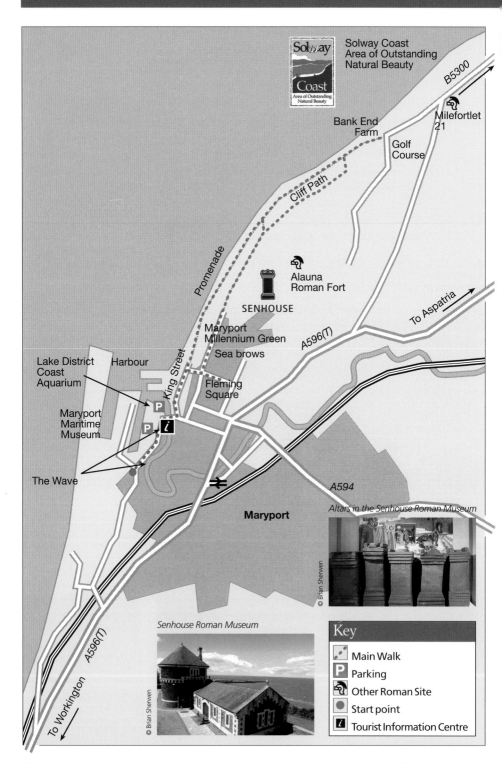

Solway Coast
Area of Outstanding
Natural Beauty

B5300

Milefortlet
21

Bank End
Farm

Golf
Course

Cliff Path

Promenade

Alauna
Roman Fort

SENHOUSE

To Aspatria

Maryport
Millennium Green

A596(T)

Sea brows

Lake District
Coast
Aquarium

Harbour

King Street

Fleming
Square

Maryport
Maritime
Museum

P

P   i

The Wave

A594

© Brian Sherwen

Maryport

Altars in the Senhouse Roman Museum

A596(T)

To Workington

Senhouse Roman Museum

© Brian Sherwen

Key

Main Walk

P Parking

Other Roman Site

Start point

i Tourist Information Centre

Roman Maryport and the Smugglers' Route

Location:
Maritime Maryport on the edge of the Solway Coast Area of Outstanding Natural Beauty

Directions
● From the Maritime Museum, cross the road and head down King Street.

● Turn right at the junction. Walk up the 109 steps, turn left at the top and walk up the grass path.

● Turn left to the sea brows and walk north away from the harbour, to reach Senhouse Roman Museum.

● Follow the hard surface path as it meanders down the sea brows. Eventually this easy-going cliff path forks. To the left, you can take a short cut back to Maryport along the promenade. If you bear right you will continue on your way over the second of three hills leading towards Bank End.

● Now turn back and begin your stroll along the long, dog-legged promenade to Maryport.

● Turn left off the promenade opposite the play area and continue along the road past the Maryport Millennium Green. Follow King Street until you arrive back at the harbour.

Highlights
- Bank End (former smugglers' cave and secret passage)
- Harbour
- Historic 18th century planned town and port
- Maritime Museum
- Promenade walks
- Senhouse Roman Museum
- The Wave Museum
- Views across the Solway Firth

Maryport Marina

© Brian Sherwen

Fleming Square, Maryport

© Brian Sherwen

Nearby attractions
- Crosscanonby Milefortlet 21
- Lake District Coast Aquarium
- Lake District National Park
- Lakeland Heavy Horse Centre
- Ravenglass/Eskdale Railway
- Solway Coast Discovery Centre (Silloth)
- The Beacon (Whitehaven)
- The Rum Story (Whitehaven)
- The Wave Museum
- Wigton
- Wood Hall Gardens

Circular walk

Distance
3 miles

Estimated walk time
1½ hours plus browsing

Grade
Easy (the path is surfaced and there is some hill walking)

Suggested start/finish
The walk begins at the Maritime Museum, near the harbour
(Grid Ref: NY 034 365)

Tourist information
Maryport Tourist Information Centre, Tel: 01900 812101 or Solway Coast Visitor Centre Tel: 016973 31944

Public transport
Journey planner enquiry line Tel: 01228 606000 Stagecoach Cumberland Tel: 01946 63222. Maryport railway station is a stop on the scenic Cumbrian Coast Line

Ordnance Survey map
Explorer (OL) 4 Keswick, Cockermouth and Wigton

Places to eat and drink
Various places to eat and drink in Maryport

Other walks in this area
Maryport Town Trails; Smugglers' Route; Start/finish of coast-to-coast long distance path at St Bees. (Enquire at Tourist Information Centre)

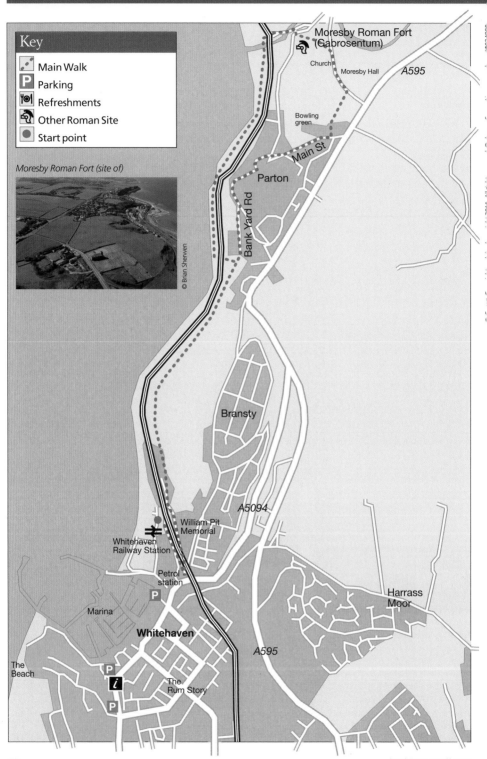

Key

- 🥾 Main Walk
- 🅿 Parking
- 🍴 Refreshments
- 🔱 Other Roman Site
- ● Start point

Moresby Roman Fort (site of)

© Brian Sherwen

Moresby Roman Fort
(Cabrosentum)

Church

Moresby Hall

A595

Bowling
green

Main St

Parton

Bank Yard Rd

Bransty

A5094

William Pit
Memorial

Whitehaven
Railway Station

Petrol
station

Harrass
Moor

🅿

Marina

Whitehaven

The
Beach

🅿

ℹ

🅿

The
Rum Story

A595

Whitehaven to Moresby Roman Fort

Location:
Coastal walk from Whitehaven

Directions
● From the railway station walk ahead to Tesco petrol station, north of Whitehaven Harbour.

● Take immediate left and within a few yards left again along the Wagon Way (cycleway signed).

● The William Pit Memorial is reached from the Wagon Way by a path to Cumbria Steelstock.

● Continue along the Wagon Way until the road to Parton is reached. Bear left and continue until school on right and village hall on left are reached.

● Take road up hill opposite village hall and continue past four bungalows on left where there is a short tarmac path through to field. Walk across old bowling green to stile, from there look for a stone wall on the right side of the field and follow wall to stile into road.

● Continue past the church entrance, after another 90 yards on left there is a tarmac path downhill. Upon reaching road cross over and turn right to small bridge over beck. Turn left and pass under railway line and re-cross beck over footbridge, keeping left along foreshore.

● Walk along foreshore path to car park. Either follow foreshore to one of the arches beyond car park or through arch beside car park to rejoin outgoing walk.

Highlights
- Historic industrial village of Parton
- Moresby Church built on the site of the Roman fort
- Moresby Hall Grade 1 listed building
- Whitehaven historic harbour and marina
- Memorial to the 1947 William Pit disaster
- Historic wagon way

Whitehaven

The End of an Era - Whitehaven

Circular walk

Distance
3 miles
Estimated walk time
2 hours
Grade
Easy (the path is surfaced and there is some hill walking)
Suggested start/finish
Whitehaven railway station (Grid Ref: NX 974 186)
Tourist information
Whitehaven Tourist Information Centre,
Tel: 01946 598914
Public transport
Whitehaven & Parton railway stations. Whitehaven railway station is a stop on the scenic Cumbrian Coast Line
Ordnance Survey map
Explorer 303 Whitehaven and Workington
Places to eat and drink
Various places in Whitehaven
Other walks in this area
Lake District National Park, start/finish of coast-to-coast long distance path at St. Bees. (Enquire at Tourist Information Centre)

© Brian Sherwen

© Brian Sherwen

Nearby attractions
- Haig Colliery Mining Museum
- Lake District National Park
- Muncaster Castle and World Owl Trust
- Ravenglass/Eskdale Railway
- Ravenglass Roman Bath House
- Senhouse Roman Museum (Maryport)
- St Bees' Beach
- The Rum Story (Whitehaven)

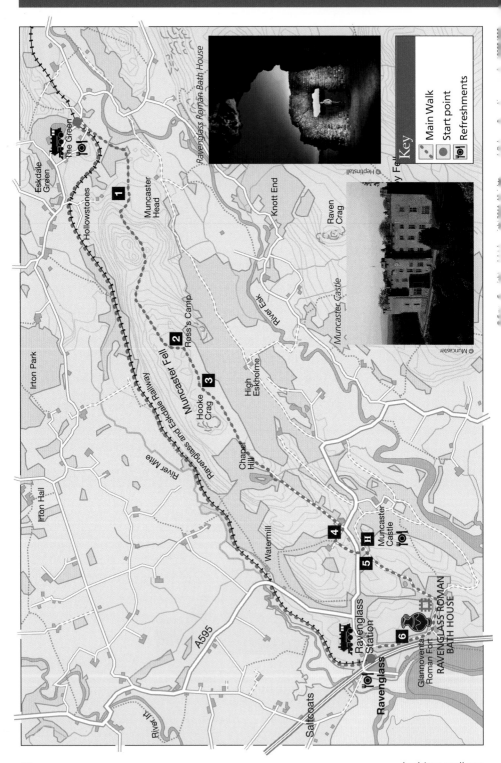

Key

- Main Walk
- Start point
- Refreshments

© Heptinstall

© Muncaster

The Green

Eskdale Green

Hollowstones

1

Muncaster Head

Ross's Camp

2

Hooke Crag

3

Knott End

Raven Crag

River Esk

High Eskholme

Muncaster Castle

Chapel Hill

Irton Park

Ravenglass and Eskdale Railway

Muncaster Fell

River Mite

Irton Hall

Watermill

4

H

Muncaster Castle

5

Ravenglass Station

6

Glannoventa Roman Fort
RAVENGLASS ROMAN BATH HOUSE

A595

Saltcoats

Ravenglass